"Ha! cursed paleface, do you dare

to enter the camp of Red Chief, the terror of the plains?"

THE RANSOM OF RED CHIEF

O.HENRY

CREATIVE EDUCATION

It looked like a good thing: but wait till I tell you. We were down South, in Alabama—Bill Driscoll and myself—when this kidnapping idea struck us. It was, as Bill afterward expressed it, "during a moment of temporary mental apparition"; but we didn't find that out till later.

There was a town down there, as flat as a flannel-cake, and called Summit, of course. It contained inhabitants of as undeleterious and self-satisfied a class of peasantry as ever clustered around a Maypole.

Bill and me had a joint capital of about six hundred dollars, and we needed just two thousand dollars more to pull off a fraudulent town-lot scheme in Western Illinois with. We talked it over on the front steps of the Hotel. Philoprogenitiveness, says we, is strong in semi-rural communities; therefore, and for other reasons, a kidnapping project ought to do better there than in the radius of newspapers that send reporters out in plain clothes to stir up talk about such things. We knew that Summit couldn't get after us with anything stronger than constables and, maybe, some lackadaisical bloodhounds and a diatribe or two in the *Weekly Farmers' Budget*. So, it looked good.

We selected for our victim the only child of a prominent citizen named Ebenezer Dorset. The father was respectable and tight, a mortgage fancier and a stern, upright collection-plate passer and forecloser. The kid was a boy of ten, with bas-relief freckles, and hair the color of the cover of the magazine you buy at the news-stand when you want to catch a train. Bill and me figured that Ebenezer would melt down for a ransom of two thousand dollars to a cent. But wait till I tell you.

About two miles from Summit was a little mountain, covered with a dense cedar brake. On the rear elevation of this mountain was a cave. There we stored provisions.

One evening after sundown, we drove in a buggy past old Dorset's house. The kid was in the street, throwing rocks at a kitten on the opposite fence.

"Hey, little boy!" says Bill, "would you like to have a bag of candy and a nice ride?"

The boy catches Bill neatly in the eye with a piece of brick.

"That will cost the old man an extra five hundred dollars," says Bill, climbing over the wheel.

That boy put up a fight like a welter-weight cinnamon bear; but, at last, we got him down in the bottom of the buggy and drove away. We took him up to the cave, and I hitched the horse in the cedar brake. After dark I drove the buggy to the little village, three miles away, where we had hired it, and walked back to the mountain.

Bill was pasting court-plaster over the scratches and bruises on his features. There was a fire burning behind the big rock at the entrance of the cave, and the boy was watching a pot of boiling coffee, with two buz-zard tail-feathers stuck in his red hair. He points a stick at me when I come up, and says:

"Ha! cursed paleface, do you dare to enter the camp of Red Chief, the terror of the plains?"

"He's all right now," says Bill, rolling up his trousers and examining some bruises on his shins. "We're playing Indian. We're making Buffalo Bill's show look like magic-lantern views of Palestine in the town hall. I'm Old Hank, the Trapper, Red Chief's captive, and I'm to be scalped at day-break. By Geronimo! that kid can kick hard."

Yes, sir, that boy seemed to be having the time of his life. The fun of camping out in a cave had made him forget that he was a captive him-self. He immediately christened me Snake-eye, the Spy, and announced that, when his braves returned from the warpath, I was to be broiled at the stake at the rising of the sun.

Then we had supper; and he filled his mouth full of bacon and bread and gravy, and began to talk. He made a during-dinner speech something like this:

"I like this fine. I never camped out before; but I had a pet 'pos-sum once, and I was nine last birthday. I hate to go to school. Rats ate up sixteen of Jimmy Talbot's aunt's speckled hen's eggs. Are there any real Indians in these woods? I want some more gravy. Does the trees moving make the wind blow? We had five puppies. What makes your nose so red, Hank? My father has lots of money. Are the stars hot? I whipped Ed Walker twice, Saturday. I don't like girls. You dassent catch toads unless with a string. Do oxen make any noise? Why are oranges round? Have you got beds to sleep on in this cave? Amos Murray has got six toes. A parrot can talk, but a monkey or a fish can't. How many does it take to make twelve?"

Every few minutes he would remember that he was a pesky redskin, and pick up his stick rifle and tiptoe to the mouth of the cave to rubber for the scouts of the hated paleface. Now and then he would let out a war-whoop that made Old Hank the Trapper shiver. That boy had Bill terrorized from the start.

"Red Chief," says I to the kid, "would you like to go home?"

"Aw, what for?" says he. "I don't have any fun at home. I hate to go to school. I like to camp out. You won't take me back home again, Snake-eye, will you?"

"Not right away," says I. "We'll stay here in the cave awhile."

"All right!" says he. "That'll be fine. I never had such fun in all my life."

We went to bed about eleven o'clock. We spread down some wide blankets and quilts and put Red Chief between us. We weren't afraid he'd run away. He kept us awake for three hours, jumping up and reaching for his rifle and screeching: "Hist! pard," in mine and Bill's ears, as the fancied crackle of a twig or the rustle of a leaf revealed to his young imagination the stealthy approach of the outlaw band. At last, I fell into a troubled sleep, and dreamed that I had been kidnapped and chained to a tree by a ferocious pirate with red hair.

Just at daybreak, I was awakened by a series of awful screams from Bill. They weren't yells, or howls, or shouts, or whoops, or yawps, such as you'd expect from a manly set of vocal organs—they were simply indecent, terrifying, humiliating screams, such as women emit when they see ghosts or caterpillars. It's an awful thing to hear a strong, desperate, fat man scream incontinently in a cave at daybreak.

I jumped up to see what the matter was. Red Chief was sitting on Bill's chest, with one hand twined in Bill's hair. In the other he had the sharp case-knife we used for slicing bacon; and he was industriously and realistically trying to take Bill's scalp, according to the sentence that had been pronounced upon him the evening before.

I got the knife away from the kid and made him lie down again. But, from that moment, Bill's spirit was broken. He laid down on his side of the bed, but he never closed an eye again in sleep as long as that boy was with us. I dozed off for a while, but along toward sun-up I remembered that Red Chief had said I was to be burned at the stake at the rising of the sun. I wasn't nervous or afraid; but I sat up and lit my pipe and leaned against a rock.

"What you getting up so soon for, Sam?" asked Bill.

"Me?" says I. "Oh, I got a kind of a pain in my shoulder. I thought sitting up would rest it."

"You're a liar!" says Bill. "You're afraid. You was to be burned at sunrise, and you was afraid he'd do it. And he would, too, if he could find a match. Ain't it awful, Sam? Do you think anybody will pay out money to get a little imp like that back home?"

"Sure," said I. "A rowdy kid like that is just the kind that parents dote on. Now, you and the Chief get up and cook breakfast, while I go up on the top of this mountain and reconnoitre."

I went up on the peak of the little mountain and ran my eye over the contiguous vicinity. Over toward Summit I expected to see the sturdy yeomanry of the village armed with scythes and pitchforks beating the countryside for the dastardly kidnappers. But what I saw was a peaceful landscape dotted with one man ploughing with a dun mule. Nobody was dragging the creek; no couriers dashed hither and yon, bringing tidings of no news to the distracted parents. There was a sylvan attitude of somnolent sleepiness pervading that section of the external outward surface of Alabama that lay exposed to my view. "Perhaps," says I to myself, "it has not yet been discovered that the wolves have borne away the tender lambkin from the fold. Heaven help the wolves!" says I, and I went down the mountain to breakfast.

When I got to the cave I found Bill backed up against the side of it, breathing hard, and the boy threatening to smash him with a rock half as big as a coconut.

"He put a red-hot boiled potato down my back," explained Bill, "and then mashed it with his foot; and I boxed his ears. Have you got a gun about you, Sam?"

I took the rock away from the boy and kind of patched up the argument. "I'll fix you," says the kid to Bill. "No man ever yet struck the Red Chief but he got paid for it. You better beware!"

After breakfast the kid takes a piece of leather with strings wrapped around it out of his pocket and goes outside the cave unwinding it.

"What's he up to now?" says Bill, anxiously. "You don't think he'll run away, do you, Sam?"

"No fear of it," says I. "He don't seem to be much of a home body. But we've got to fix up some plan about the ransom. There don't seem to be much excitement around Summit on account of his disappearance; but maybe they haven't realized yet that he's gone. His folks may think he's spending the night with Aunt Jane or one of the neighbors. Anyhow, he'll be missed to-day. To-night we must get a message to his father demanding the two thousand dollars for his return."

Just then we heard a kind of war-whoop, such as David might have emitted when he knocked out the champion Goliath. It was a sling that Red Chief had pulled out of his pocket, and he was whirling it around his head.

I dodged, and heard a heavy thud and a kind of a sigh from Bill, like a horse gives out when you take his saddle off. A niggerhead rock the size of an egg had caught Bill just behind his left ear. He loosened himself all over and fell in the fire across the frying pan of hot water for washing the dishes. I dragged him out and poured cold water on his head for half an hour.

By and by, Bill sits up and feels behind his ear and says: "Sam, do you know who my favorite Biblical character is?"

"Take it easy," says I. "You'll come to your senses presently."

"King Herod," says he. "You won't go away and leave me here alone, will you, Sam?"

I went out and caught that boy and shook him until his freckles rattled.

"If you don't behave," says I, "I'll take you straight home. Now, are you going to be good, or not?"

"I was only funning," says he, sullenly. "I didn't mean to hurt Old Hank. But what did he hit me for? I'll behave, Snake-eye, if you won't send me home, and if you'll let me play the Black Scout to-day."

"I don't know the game," says I. "That's for you and Mr. Bill to decide. He's your playmate for the day. I'm going away for a while, on business. Now, you come in and make friends with him and say you are sorry for hurting him, or home you go, at once."

I made him and Bill shake hands, and then I took Bill aside and told him I was going to Poplar Grove, a little village three miles from the cave, and find out what I could about how the kidnapping had been regarded in Summit. Also, I thought it best to send a peremptory letter to old man Dorset that day, demanding the ransom and dictating how it should be paid.

"You know, Sam," says Bill, "I've stood by you without batting an eye in earthquakes, fire, and flood—in poker games, dynamite outrages, police raids, train robberies, and cyclones. I never lost my nerve yet till we kidnapped that two-legged skyrocket of a kid. He's got me going. You won't leave me long with him, will you, Sam?"

"I'll be back some time this afternoon," says I. "You must keep the boy amused and quiet till I return. And now we'll write the letter to old Dorset."

Bill and I got paper and pencil and worked on the letter while Red Chief, with a blanket wrapped around him, strutted up and down, guarding the mouth of the cave. Bill begged me tearfully to make the ransom fifteen hundred dollars instead of two thousand. "I ain't attempting," says he, "to decry the celebrated moral aspect of parental affection, but we're dealing with humans, and it ain't human for anybody to give up two thousand dollars for that forty-pound chunk of freckled wildcat. I'm willing to take a chance at fifteen hundred dollars. You can charge the difference up to me."

So, to relieve Bill, I acceded, and we collaborated a letter that ran this way:

Ebenezer Dorset, Esq.:

We have your boy concealed in a place far from Summit. It is useless for you or the most skilful detectives to attempt to find him. Absolutely, the only terms on which you can have him restored to you are these: We demand fifteen hundred dollars in large bills for his return; the money to be left at midnight to-night at the same spot and in the same box as your reply—as hereinafter described. If you agree to these terms, send your answer in writing by a solitary messenger to-night at half-past eight o'clock. After crossing Owl Creek, on the road to Poplar Grove, there are three large trees about a hundred yards apart, close to the fence of the wheat field on the right-hand side. At the bottom of the fence-post, opposite the third tree, will be found a small pasteboard box.

The messenger will place the answer in this box and return immediately to Summit.

If you attempt any treachery or fail to comply with our demand as stated, you will never see your boy again.

If you pay the money as demanded, he will be returned to you safe and well within three hours. These terms are final, and if you do not accede to them no further communication will be attempted.

Two Desperate Men

I addressed this letter to Dorset, and put it in my pocket. As I was about to start, the kid comes up to me and says:

"Aw, Snake-eye, you said I could play the Black Scout while you was gone."

"Play it, of course," says I. "Mr. Bill will play with you. What kind of a game is it?"

"I'm the Black Scout," says Red Chief, "and I have to ride to the stockade to warn the settlers that the Indians are coming. I'm tired of playing Indian myself. I want to be the Black Scout."

"All right," says I. "It sounds harmless to me. I guess Mr. Bill will help you foil the pesky savages."

"What am I to do?" asks Bill, looking at the kid suspiciously.

"You are the hoss," says Black Scout. "Get down on your hands and knees. How can I ride to the stockade without a hoss?"

"You'd better keep him interested," said I, "till we get the scheme going. Loosen up."

Bill gets down on his all fours, and a look comes in his eye like a rabbit's when you catch it in a trap.

"How far is it to the stockade, kid?" he asks, in a husky manner of voice.

"Ninety miles," says the Black Scout. "And you have to hump yourself to get there on time. Whoa, now!"

The Black Scout jumps on Bill's back and digs his heels in his side.

"For Heaven's sake," says Bill, "hurry back, Sam, as soon as you can. I wish we hadn't made the ransom more than a thousand. Say, you quit kicking me or I'll get up and warm you good."

I walked over to Poplar Grove and sat around the post office and store, talking with the chaw-bacons that came in to trade. One whiskerando says that he hears Summit is all upset on account of Elder Ebenezer Dorset's boy having been lost or stolen. That was all I wanted to know. I bought some smoking tobacco, referred casually to the price of black-eyed peas, posted my letter surreptitiously, and came away. The postmaster said the mail-carrier would come by in an hour to take the mail to Summit.

When I got back to the cave Bill and the boy were not to be found. I explored the vicinity of the cave, and risked a yodel or two, but there was no response.

So I lighted my pipe and sat down on a mossy bank to await developments.

In about half an hour I heard the bushes rustle, and Bill wabbled out into the little glade in front of the cave. Behind him was the kid, stepping softly like a scout, with a broad grin on his face. Bill stopped, took off his hat, and wiped his face with a red handkerchief. The kid stopped about eight feet behind him.

"Sam," says Bill, "I suppose you'll think I'm a renegade, but I couldn't help it. I'm a grown person with masculine proclivities and habits of self-defense, but there is a time when all systems of egotism and pre-dominance fail. The boy is gone. I have sent him home. All is off. There was martyrs in old times," goes on Bill, "that suffered death rather than give up the particular graft they enjoyed. None of 'em ever was subjugat-ed to such supernatural tortures as I have been. I tried to be faithful to our articles of depredation; but there came a limit."

"What's the trouble, Bill?" I asks him.

"I was rode," says Bill, "the ninety miles to the stockade, not barring an inch. Then, when the settlers was rescued, I was given oats. Sand ain't a palatable substitute. And then, for an hour I had to try to explain to him why there was nothin' in holes, how a road can run both ways, and what makes the grass green. I tell you, Sam, a human can only stand so much. I takes him by the neck of his clothes and drags him down the mountain. On the way he kicks my legs black and blue from the knees down; and I've got to have two or three bites on my thumb and hand cauterized.

"But he's gone"—continues Bill—"gone home. I showed him the road to Summit and kicked him about eight feet nearer there at one kick. I'm sorry we lose the ransom; but it was either that or Bill Driscoll to the madhouse."

Bill is puffing and blowing, but there is a look of ineffable peace and growing content on his rose-pink features.

"Bill," says I, "there isn't any heart disease in your family, is there?"

"No," says Bill, "nothing chronic except malaria and accidents. Why?"

"Then you might turn around," says I, "and have a look behind you."

Bill turns and sees the boy, and loses his complexion and sits down plump on the ground and begins to pluck aimlessly at grass and little sticks. For an hour I was afraid for his mind. And then I told him that my scheme was to put the whole job through immediately and that we would get the ransom and be off with it by midnight if old Dorset fell in with our proposition. So Bill braced up enough to give the kid a weak sort of a smile and a promise to play the Russian in a Japanese war with him as soon as he felt a little better.

I had a scheme for collecting that ransom without danger of being caught by counterplots that ought to commend itself to professional kidnappers. The tree under which the answer was to be left—and the money later on—was close to the road fence with big, bare fields on all sides. If a gang of constables should be watching for any one to come for the note, they could see him a long way off crossing the fields or in the road. But no, sirree! At half-past eight I was up in that tree as well hidden as a tree toad, waiting for the messenger to arrive.

Exactly on time, a half-grown boy rides up the road on a bicycle, locates the pasteboard box at the foot of the fencepost, slips a folded piece of paper into it, and pedals away again back toward Summit.

I waited an hour and then concluded the thing was square. I slid down the tree, got the note, slipped along the fence till I struck the woods, and was back at the cave in another half an hour. I opened the note, got near the lantern, and read it to Bill. It was written with a pen in a crabbed hand, and the sum and substance of it was this:

Two Desperate Men,

Gentlemen: I received your letter to-day by post, in regard to the ransom you ask for the return of my son. I think you are a little high in your demands, and I hereby make you a counter-proposition, which I am inclined to believe you will accept. You bring Johnny home and pay me two hundred and fifty dollars in cash, and I agree to take him off your hands. You had better come at night, for the neighbors believe he is lost, and I couldn't be responsible for what they would do to anybody they saw bringing him back.

Very respectfully,

Ebenezer Dorset

"Great pirates of Penzance!" says I; "of all the impudent—"

But I glanced at Bill, and hesitated. He had the most appealing look in his eyes I ever saw on the face of a dumb or a talking brute.

"Sam," says he, "what's two hundred and fifty dollars, after all? We've got the money. One more night of this kid will send me to a bed in Bedlam. Besides being a thorough gentleman, I think Mr. Dorset is a spendthrift for making us such a liberal offer. You ain't going to let the chance go, are you?"

"Tell you the truth, Bill," says I, "this little he ewe lamb has somewhat got on my nerves too. We'll take him home, pay the ransom, and make our getaway."

We took him home that night. We got him to go by telling him that his father had bought a silver-mounted rifle and a pair of moccasins for him, and we were going to hunt bears the next day.

It was just twelve o'clock when we knocked at Ebenezer's front door. Just at the moment when I should have been abstracting the fifteen hundred dollars from the box under the tree, according to the original proposition, Bill was counting out two hundred and fifty dollars into Dorset's hand.

When the kid found out we were going to leave him at home he started up a howl like a calliope and fastened himself as tight as a leech to Bill's leg. His father peeled him away gradually, like a porous plaster.

"How long can you hold him?" asks Bill.

"I'm not as strong as I used to be," says old Dorset, "but I think I can promise you ten minutes."

"Enough," says Bill. "In ten minutes I shall cross the Central, Southern, and Middle Western States, and be legging it trippingly for the Canadian border."

And, as dark as it was, and as fat as Bill was, and as good a runner as I am, he was a good mile and a half out of Summit before I could catch up with him.

A CLOSER LOOK

O. Henry was a masterful storyteller. He knew how to tell a story, and he knew how to tell it well. His stories had a set pattern from which he rarely deviated, but the best O. Henry stories were not merely formulaic; they were unpredictable because they also included ironic twists and surprise endings. The man who wrote more than 600 stories—most of them within the last 10 years of his life—had plenty of practice in perfecting his art by the time he published a volume called *Whirligigs* in 1910. "The Ransom of Red Chief," one of the tales found in *Whirligigs*, eventually became one of his best-known stories and one of the finest examples of the definitive O. Henry style.

Like all good storytellers, Henry approached a story's beginning with the determined intention of hooking his readers and making them want to read on. From the outset of "The Ransom of Red Chief," the reader knows that all is not as it seems: "It looked like a good thing: but wait till I tell you," confides the narrator, Sam (5). Once more, before he gets on with the story of the kidnapping, Sam uses the words "but wait till I tell you" to warn the reader against making hasty judgments. This, of course, ensures that the person reading the tale will be enticed into doing just that and will wrongly assume that this tale is like any other kidnapping story—which is precisely the effect Henry desired.

The kidnapping motif is the overarching theme of the story, and from that stems the dominant source of irony and tension, for this is no ordinary kidnapping narrative. All of the ironic elements Henry uses produce a tension that mounts throughout the story until everything is allowed to come back together to form a greater, more perfect resolution than would have seemed possible in the beginning. There is nothing extraneous in "The Ransom"; everything fits together to create a coherent whole—especially the parts that seem out of joint.

Henry starts small to achieve his grand goal. The first example of irony is minor: the Alabama town around which the action is centered is called Summit, which is "as flat as a flannel-cake" (5). The next instance of irony is somewhat more subtle. The kidnappers, Bill and Sam, are not typical "bad guys"; kidnapping does not seem to be their chosen profession. Their elevated diction, apparent in such words as "undeleterious," "philoprogenitiveness," and "lackadaisical" is evidence that these are not uneducated men, but it causes one to wonder how they acquired such a vocabulary. In the same sentence as "philoprogenitiveness" is the ungrammatical construction "says we," adding to the "villains" an even greater air of falseness or amateurship (5).

On the other hand, Henry uses diction elsewhere to reflect the lifelike and natural voice of the child who is the title character. The captive, who proclaims himself "Red Chief," rambles on in a monologue that runs the gamut from his background, his observations, and his likes and dislikes, to his insatiable questions: "'I like this fine. I never camped out before; but I had a pet 'possum once, and I was nine last birthday. I hate to go to school. Rats ate up sixteen of Jimmy Talbot's aunt's speckled hen's eggs. Are there any real Indians in these woods? I want some more gravy'" (7). The bouncy train of thought is characteristic of an energetic child's pattern of speech, and Henry uses such speech to make the boy seem believable, not to mention entertaining.

Yet Red Chief does not think of himself as a victim. In a reversal of roles, it is the kidnappers who are made miserable by the antics of their prisoner, even in their dreams (9). Increasingly frightened by the boy who is supposed to be their victim, Sam and Bill use the threat of sending him home to keep his wild temper under control: "'Now, you come in and make friends with him and say you are sorry for hurting him, or home you go, at once'" (13). Instead of the boy being punished by being held captive, it is the kidnappers who are penalizing themselves.

In the culminating instance of irony, Henry uses the standard convention of the ransom letter in order to follow the set pattern of a kidnapping tale, but the captive's father does not reply in an appropriate manner: instead of agreeing to the terms set by the kidnappers, he bargains them down, and Henry has his twist: "'You bring Johnny home and pay me two hundred and fifty dollars in cash, and I agree to take him off your hands'" (19–20). Bill and Sam, who really are "two desperate men" by that point, have to bribe the child in order to get him to go back home, and once they deposit the boy and the money, the criminals have to run out of town to escape the clutches not of the police but of Red Chief, "the terror of the plains."

O. Henry, pictured around 1904

ABOUT THE AUTHOR

O. Henry was born William Sydney Porter on September 11, 1862, in Greensboro, North Carolina. The son of a physician, Porter worked in his uncle's drugstore for five years and became a licensed pharmacist when he was 19. Seeking more adventure on the frontier, he moved to Texas, where he worked on ranches, as a bank clerk, and tried his hand at journalism, learning to speak Spanish along the way. In 1887, he married a wealthy woman named Athol Estes, and of their two children, only their daughter Margaret survived infancy.

For the next four years, the Porter family lived simply but happily in Austin, Texas, and Porter began writing stories for national magazines. Soon, the enterprising Porter started up a weekly magazine called *The Rolling Stone*, which showcased humorous stories and cartoons of his own creation. The venture was not successful, however, and Porter soon began writing for the *Houston Post* instead, supplementing his pay by serving as a teller at the First National Bank of Austin.

The year that changed Porter's life was 1896: after being accused of stealing money from the bank, Porter fled to Honduras by way of New Orleans and hid in Central America until 1897, when he heard that Athol, still in Texas, was close to death from her struggle with tuberculosis. Upon returning to the U.S., Porter was convicted of embezzlement and sentenced to serve five years at the Ohio State Penitentiary in Columbus. During his three-year stay (1898–1901), abbreviated because of his good behavior, he worked at the prison pharmacy, sleeping on a cot in the hospital, and gathered story material from his fellow inmates. He came to know hardened criminals who had committed grisly crimes, and he learned about men who wanted a chance to change their ways. He then started writing and selling those stories to magazines to help support his young daughter, using the pseudonym "O. Henry." (Some biographers believe that he took the name from a prison warden named Orrin Henry, while others think that he took his inspiration from a well-known French pharmacist, Etienne-Ossian Henry.)

O. Henry emerged from prison an established and popular author. Henry wanted to distance himself as much as possible from the man who had been imprisoned, so he moved to New York City in 1902 and immediately began to write about the people of that metropolis. Many of his best-known stories were inspired by New York, and Henry came to identify strongly with its people and places. "There are stories in everything," he once claimed. "I've got some of my best yarns from park benches, lampposts, and newspaper stands." Those "yarns" quickly cemented his reputation as a gifted short-story author. He used his experiences in Central

America as a backdrop for his first collection of tales, *Cabbages and Kings*, in 1904.

Two years later, Henry's stories about *The Four Million* people of New York appeared. This collection included the popular, heart-rending Christmas story "The Gift of the Magi," about a poor young couple's unfortunate gift-giving experience. From then on, Porter continued to hone his craft and sharpen his wit, and the name O. Henry soon became synonymous with surprise endings or plots that had a clever twist.

Porter's first biographer, C. Alphonso Smith, described the classic O. Henry short story structure as having four stages, which corresponded with the stages in his life. First comes the "arresting beginning," the hook to lure the reader. The next stage presents the "rising action," during which the reader begins to make assumptions about how the story will end. Then comes the climax, and the reader realizes that all is not what he or she had supposed. Finally, the fourth stage presents the conclusion with a twist, surprising the reader with an unforeseen but believable ending. One of the most famous stories to utilize such a twist was "The Ransom of Red Chief," first published in 1910 as part of a volume called *Whirligigs*.

He may have been a masterful storyteller, but Henry's life was not a fairy tale of happiness. He struggled with alcoholism, poor health, and

A New York City street, 1909

financial issues in the later years of his life, always on the cusp of bank-ruptcy and serious illness. His second marriage in 1907 lasted only two years, and the 47-year-old Henry died of cirrhosis of the liver on June 5, 1910, in the city he loved best: New York. "Pull up the shades so I can see New York," were reportedly his last words. "I don't want to go home in the dark." Three collections of short stories were published after his death, and in 1919, the first O. Henry Award (for outstanding short-story writing) was given. O. Henry, the writer with a rare gift for crafting tales of human inter-est, continues to be honored today—in New York and throughout the world.

Published by Creative Education

P.O. Box 227, Mankato, Minnesota 56002

Creative Education is an imprint of The Creative Company.

Design by Rita Marshall; production by Heidi Thompson

Page 22–31 text by Kate Riggs

Printed in the United States of America

Photographs by Corbis (Bettman), Getty Images (Edward Steichen)

Library of Congress Cataloging-in-Publication Data

Henry, O., 1862–1910.

The ransom of Red Chief / by O. Henry.

p. cm. – (Creative short stories)

ISBN 978-1-58341-585-6

I. Title. II. Series.

PS2649.P5R36 2007

813'.52–dc22   2007008488

First edition

2 4 6 8 9 7 5 3 1